VAN PELT

secrets of
sanity for
**stressed
women**

First published 2008
Copyright © 2008
All rights reserved. No part of this publication
may be reproduced in any form without prior
permission from the publisher.
British Library Cataloguing in Publication Data.
Catalogue record for this book is available from
the British Library.

ISBN: 978-1-906381-03-5

Published by Autumn House Limited,
Grantham, Lincolnshire

Printed in Thailand

Bible versions used:
NLT = *New Living Translation*
NIV = *New International Version*
KJV = *King James Version*
NRSV = *New Revised Standard Version*
RSV = *Revised Standard Version*
TLB = *The Living Bible*
MGE = *The Message Bible*

Affirmation

Today I choose to put order in my life.

I will ignore negative, self-defeating
messages from the past.

I can and will begin doing things in a fitting
and orderly manner – and it can be fun!

The first step

When you commit yourself fully to a new way
of doing things, when you take the first step,
you make it possible for God to make you
the person he intended. He can bring out
strengths you didn't know you had. It is
possible for you to surprise yourself
continually and live in a constant state
of exhilaration and self-discovery.

That is what growing is all about.

Four biblical principles

To be a new woman you need to get on top of four biblical principles:

1. Do everything in an orderly manner.
2. Do things well.
3. Have a joyful spirit.
4. Be motivated to achieve your goal.

1. Do everything in an orderly manner

'Let all things be done decently and in order.'
1 Corinthians 14:40, KJV

Powerful words! Words that should guide us daily in everything we do. Wherever we are – at home or at work – do everything in an orderly manner. Have a method and a system, a procedure, for accomplishing the tasks of the day.

2. Do things well

*'Whatever your hand finds
to do, do it with
all your might.'*
Ecclesiastes 9:10, NIV

Whatever task we attempt, wherever we are,
and whoever we are doing it for, it should be
done well. This means we will take care to
complete our daily task satisfactorily and
properly.

If it is worth doing at all, it must be done
correctly. Let us strive for excellence in
everything we attempt.

3. Have a joyful spirit

'Rejoice in the Lord alway:
and again I say, Rejoice.'
Philippians 4:4, KJV

While we are getting things orderly, attempting to do things well, and striving for excellence, we must watch our attitude. An interesting verse in Philippians 2 admonishes us to *do all things without murmurings'* (verse 14, KJV).

Having a joyful spirit while we complete our tasks brings a satisfaction and contentment that results in delight and gladness.

4. Be motivated to achieve your goal

'But one thing I do: Forgetting what is behind and straining towards what is ahead, I press towards the goal to win the prize for which God has called me heavenward in Christ Jesus.'
Philippians 3:13, NIV.

Secret of contentment

'I can do everything through him
who gives me strength.'
Philippians 4:13, NIV

Now is the time to forget how often you have
tried and failed. Forget the I-can't-handle-it
attitudes! Paul focused on what he was
supposed to do, not on past failures. He
had his priorities straight and was grateful
for everything God had given him.

An empty place

Often the desire for more and better possessions and bigger and greater homes is really a longing to fill an empty place in one's life. True contentment in life is found by examining your perspective of 'things', sorting through your priorities, knowing where your source of strength lies.

Sufficient power

Christ does not grant us superhuman ability
to accomplish anything we can imagine, but
we can receive power sufficient to do his will
and to face the challenges of our daily tasks.
Through each task and time pressure, ask
Christ to strengthen you.

No more excuses

Getting a home 'decent and in order' has to do with establishing good habits, rather than constantly caving in to a multitude of excuses why you can't get it together at home.

Twenty-one days to better habits

Regardless of a person's age or gender, it takes 21-45 days to change a habit. An idea or action must be repeated for twenty-one consecutive days before it becomes permanently fixed in the subconscious.

Holding Pattern

If you have lost control of your time, or if your life is in a holding pattern, you are malfunctioning. You may be much like a pilot who announced to his passengers, 'We're lost, folks; but cheer up – we're making excellent headway.'

The Bible says,
'Let everyone be sure that [she]
is doing [her] very best.'
Galatians 6:4, TLB

Sense of direction

A sense of direction can make the
difference between responsible living and
simply surviving with a group of boarders
who happen to be your family. Having a plan
puts you in control. Add organisational skills
to your plan, and you have the ingredients
for vitality and purposeful living.

Stay open to new ideas

4+4, 5+3, 6+2, 7+1, and 8+0, all equal 8.

Stay open to new ways of solving old dilemmas.

One day at a time

You can change one small area of your life at a time, one day at a time. Success and growth come from a series of small changes that lead towards the goal you have set for yourself. It's never too late to start; it's never too late to change!

Home

'Unless the Lord builds the house, those
who build it labour in vain.'
Psalm 127:1, NRSV

'This is the true nature of home – it is the
place of peace; the shelter not only from
injury, but from all terror, doubt and division.'
John Ruskin

Time to commit

It has been said that most of us use only one tenth of the power to act that God has granted us. By committing ourselves to a new course of action, we begin drawing on the other 90%. You can achieve anything God puts in your mind as a goal.

'This one thing I do: forgetting what lies behind and straining forward to what lies ahead, I press on toward the goal for the prize.'
Philippians 3:13, 14, NRSV

Settled plans

'Commit your works to the Lord,
and your plans will be established.'
Proverbs 16:3, RSV

If your plans are established, you do not
need to become discouraged or frustrated,
even when things do not progress as you
want them to.

You know you are doing what God wants.

Visualise success

Begin to visualise yourself as a success.

If you want to become better organised,
picture yourself as an organised person.
Let your mind dwell on the advantages of
being better organised, rather than on how
difficult it will be to accomplish this task.

Visualise yourself successfully moving
through the day, efficiently completing
each task before you.

Be surrounded
with positives

Spend less time talking on the phone to
friends who want to gossip or hash over their
troubles. Watch the way you talk to family
members and friends. Avoid negative thinking.

Turn off TV soap operas. Soap operas glorify
the lives of pathetic people, who are either
just getting out of trouble or heading back
into it.

Oceans
of fantasy

Do not drown beneath oceans of TV
fantasy. Focusing attention on much trouble
becomes addictive and robs you of time.

Clear your mind of negativity.

Make sure TV does not add to your stress.

Be patient

Refuse to accept negative thoughts about yourself or of what you can accomplish. Replace all negative thoughts with positive ones.

Disorder affects every area of your life. It can ruin a good marriage and douse any hope for a troubled marriage. Your finances, social life, and everything are affected by disorder.

Affirmation

Each day repeat the affirmation
on page 3.

In the beginning, celebrate every
improvement made, regardless
of how small.

Concentrate on your new direction.

Consult your Divine Partner daily

Prayer is the mortar that holds your home together.

Daily devotions

*'A hundred men make an encampment,
but it takes a woman to make a home.'*
Chinese proverb

And a woman builds her home on her daily
devotions. She consults her Divine Partner
through prayer and Bible study. These are of
tremendous advantage as you set priorities.

A woman who lays her daily plans before the
Master Planner usually has her priorities
straight.

Self-defeating habits

Prayer helps control self-defeating habits, attitudes, and impulsive patterns of behaviour. Prayer increases faith in your ability to achieve your goals of decency and order. Prayer gives strength to endure frustrations, stress, and occasional failures.

Prayer notebook

Keep a prayer notebook in which you write
down your prayer requests and the answers
God gives you.

This will deepen your faith in God as you
track his leading in your life.

Eyes on the goal

We must keep our eyes on our goal –
and on any small successes.

Do not be swallowed up by failures.

Challenges

You can be like the person who is afraid of water and, when seeing a large wave coming in their direction, panics and runs, only to be caught, knocked down, and crushed by the rushing water.

Or

You can be like the surfer who anticipates the giant wave, prepares to meet it, rises above it, and rides with its forces to victory!

Prioritise!

When dealing with challenges you need to learn to prioritise.

The common-sense procedure to maintaining a home is to put first things first and get your mornings under control. The woman who never gets anything done, who is always behind, must break old habits and learn new ones.

Organise!

*'Organising is what you do before you do
something, so that when you do it, it's
not all mixed up.'*
Christopher Robin in *Winnie the Pooh*
by A. A. Milne

Planning:
a key to sanity

Set realistic goals that can be carried out.
A multitude of activities and tasks, great and
small, become the stairway to your Personal
Daily Plan.

First we must slow ourselves down long
enough to map out the plan on paper. This
can be done in 30-60 minutes. Take a lunch
hour, get up early one morning, or take a few
minutes after the kids are in bed to map out a
plan that you think might work for your week.

Five steps for creating your own PDP (Personal Daily Plan)

Step 1. Fill in regular appointments and activities.

Step 2. Assign one major task to each weekday.

Step 3. Assign 3-5 mini tasks to each major daily task.

Step 4. Choose a time for major tasks that best suits you.

Step 5. Schedule important things.

Step 1: Fill in regular appointments and activities

Begin by filling in regularly scheduled events, appointments and activities for the forthcoming week. Write in mealtimes and regular appointments such as music lessons, dental/doctor appointments, sports practices, Pathfinder meetings, prayer meetings, work hours, rising and retiring times.

Step 2: Assign one major task to each weekday

A major task is anything that takes more than 15 minutes to do. Major tasks differ from mini tasks in time only. Major tasks include such things as cleaning the kitchen, vacuuming, dusting, grocery shopping, laundry and bathrooms.

Step 3: Assign 3-5 mini tasks to each major daily task

For example, when I go into the kitchen on Monday to do my major task, it would make sense to concentrate on mini tasks while I'm there. Some of these might include cleaning the inside of the microwave, cleaning the outside of the microwave, cleaning the outside of the fridge, cleaning the top of the fridge, cleaning the appliances (toaster, blender, mixer).

Adding 3-5 mini tasks to the major task of the day adds 9-15 minutes, still a cumulative total of only 40-45 minutes for this day. Wednesday's mini tasks generally focus on the bathroom area — cleaning light fittings, windows; polishing cabinets, reorganising drawers.

Step 4: Choose a time for major tasks that best suits you

Stick to schedule. Don't on an impulse go shopping.

Before you do anything else, prioritise the tasks assigned for the day.

Step 5: Schedule important things

Your PDP needs to include important things like personal devotions and exercise. If these are a priority in your life, they will not be crowded out by other more urgent things clamouring for your attention.

'Routine' is not a dirty word

On the contrary, it is the key to an organised life. Establishing a routine that works for you and your family won't happen overnight. It is a gradual process. There are morning, afternoon, evening and even weekend routines.

So that your entire day is not thrown, the most important routine to get right is your morning routine.

Stressors

The biggest morning stressors are:
1. Too many things to do in too little time.
2. Arguments with children over what clothing to wear to school.
3. Last-minute signatures needed on school papers.
4. Lunches not ready; can't find lunch money.
5. Hunting for something needed for a schoolboy's backpack.

Establishing a routine can turn morning madness into orderly peace.

The night before . . .

- Tidy up the house.

- Set the table for breakfast.

- Prepare packed lunches.

- Select clothing and lay it out.

Morning discipline

'Start with God – the first step in learning
is bowing down to God; only fools thumb
their noses at such wisdom and learning.'
Proverbs 1:7, MGE

'Fear of the Lord is the beginning of
knowledge. Only fools despise wisdom
and discipline.'
Proverbs 1:7, NLT

- Schedule family mealtimes. It will simplify planning and preparation if there is a weekly routine of meals.
- Make dinner enjoyable by encouraging the children to tell about their day.
- Share responsibility for dinner preparation, and clearing up after the meal.
- Schedule a few minutes of fun time with the family several times a week.
- Create a routine for homework in an environment free from too many interruptions.

Be flexible

You designed your PDP around
essential tasks, but allow a time cushion
for emergencies that come up, or for those
times when you are exhausted. Just as
planning is key to time management, so
flexibility is the key to good planning.

Take breaks!

Studies on work habits show that productivity
goes up and accidents go down when workers
take a periodic break from their labours. The
same is true in the home. Write personal time
into your PDP.

Plan to succeed!

It is possible to get more done in less time once you get your PDP functioning.

Failing to plan is planning to fail.

The problem?

The house is a disaster area, with a barely discernable pathway leading towards the bedroom. Bedroom door barely cracks open against a heap of clothes tossed wherever, scattered toys, laundry, shoes, and a host of other unmentionables. Your nerves are frazzled and your temper is short. You have to take a day off work and rent a bulldozer to find floor level.

The five-minute miracle

There is another way. Here's how it
works. Before leaving for work or school
or beginning your duties for the day, devote
five minutes to straightening each room
before you leave it. Where to begin?
I suggest the bathroom.

Avoid the tendency to deep-clean

The five-minute miracle isn't the time to scrub and polish the kitchen floor, clean out the fridge, shampoo carpets, or clean the hall cupboard.

Designate several tidying up periods throughout the day.

Keep up!

Remember: keeping up is easier than catching up. Avoid feeling so defeated by a tornado-struck room that you do nothing. The room may look as if it will take hours to restore order, but a few minutes' tidying time will keep it from getting worse.

Prayer

Home is not given, but made.
Father, light up the small duties of this day.
May they shine with the beauty of your
    presence.
May I find glory in the small common tasks
    before me. Amen.

Tracking weekly activities

The first thing a personal planner must have is a calendar. Since we don't have multiple appointments every hour of the day, a week-at-a-glance calendar will do.

On Sunday night or Monday morning map out all appointments for the forthcoming week.

Whenever you write down an appointment, lunch date, or meeting on your calendar, include a phone number for future reference should you need to cancel or reschedule.

Phone numbers

Keep a list of all useful phone numbers. Include in the list your doctor's and dentist's surgeries.

Keep a careful record of all prescription drugs you are on.

Have a page for dietary and nutritional information.

The last section of the planner contains the name, address and phone number of all personal friends A-Z.

The cardinal rule for using a personal planner is: Never leave home without it!

Here are a few things your planner can be extended to track:

1. A reminder section for doing household chores.
2. A page to write down gift ideas as they come to mind.
3. Menu plans.
4. Spiritual insights.
5. Weekly 'to do' items.
6. A self-check system for developing and evaluating annual or life goals.

Control centre

Every home needs a control centre. These are the necessary supplies: a phone, a notice board for messages, a big calendar, a filing cabinet or box, drawing pins, cellotape, a ruler, rubber bands, glue, a stapler, scissors, letter trays for filing and organising papers, paper clips, pens, pencils and markers, paper and envelopes, stamps, post-it notes, phone directories and a calculator.

Commit

*'Commit to the Lord whatever you do,
and your plans will succeed.'*
Proverbs 16:3, NIV

*'You will keep in perfect peace all who
trust in you, all whose thoughts are fixed
on you!'*
Isaiah 26:3, NLT

The ideal wife

'Who can find a virtuous and capable wife?
She is more precious than rubies.
Her husband can trust her,
And she will greatly enrich his life.
She brings him good, not harm,
All the days of her life.'
Proverbs 31:10-12, NLT

An ideal
wife too far?

'She finds wool and flax
and busily spins it.
She is like a merchant's ship,
bringing her food from afar.
She gets up before dawn to prepare
breakfast for her household
And plan the day's work for her servant girl.'
Proverbs 31:13-15, NLT

The career wife

'She goes to inspect a field and buys it;
with her earnings she plants a vineyard.
She is energetic and strong,
a hard worker.
She makes sure her dealings are profitable;
her lamp burns late into the night.
Her hands are busy spinning thread,
her fingers twisting fibre.
She extends a helping hand to the poor
and opens her arms to the needy.'
Proverbs 31:17-20, NLT

More on
the ideal wife

'She is clothed with strength and dignity,
and she laughs without fear of the future.
When she speaks, her words are wise,
and she gives instruction with kindness.
She carefully watches everything in her
household and suffers nothing from laziness.
Her children stand and bless her.
Her husband praises her:
"There are many virtuous and capable
women in the world but you surpass them all!"'
Proverbs 31:25-29, NLT

Menu planning

If you serve two meals a day, it means you plan, cook and clean up after 700 meals a year. It's an exhausting ordeal being a full-time home-maker!

Regain
recipe control

Make life easier for yourself and save
countless hours of mental stewing by
planning menus in advance. In order to
menu-plan in an organised manner, all
loose recipes must be stored in a card file.
Categorise them under *beverages, main
dishes, vegetables, salads, desserts,* etc.

Recipe book

Why not buy a three-ring recipe book? Select twenty of your family's favourite main dishes.

Menu-planning can take 10-30 minutes or more, depending upon your temperament.

Save every menu plan for the first six weeks. After that it becomes a breeze to recycle menus, making slight adaptations.

Quick and easy meal-planning ideas

- Have a crock-pot night: toss a soup mix into the crock-pot before you begin your day. By 5pm the smell of simmering soup should be wafting through the house. A fresh salad (from a salad mix, if you prefer) and a tasty bread will complete one easy and nutritious meal.
- Make Friday night special by planning a family favourite.
- Order take-away food one night a week.
- Have older children and/or your husband plan and prepare a meal one night a week.

Prepare a shopping list

When planning, keep in mind family preferences and let them dictate, or at least influence, your choices.

Impulse buying is the best way to sabotage a food budget. Shop with your list in your hand, and there will be fewer decisions to make at the store.

Menu planning and grocery shopping should be done at the same time of the week.

Men in the kitchen

If you work full time outside the home and are married to a man who is yet to learn how to do more than come to the table when called, it's time to act! Call a powwow between the two of you. Inform your spouse that you can no longer handle planning and preparing meals every night of the week, and you need help. Unless he volunteers, tell him that you need his help for at least one night a week.

Kids in
the kitchen

A survey of working mothers shows that
77% prepare dinner alone, and 64% handle
clearing up alone. This is wrong. Children
need to be involved in the menu planning,
food preparation, and clearing up. This is a
great time for parent and child to work side
by side.

Likes and dislikes

Avoid making a big deal over food likes and dislikes. Attention to food dislikes sets up bad feelings. If a certain food has not been eaten by the end of a normal mealtime, remove the plate without comment. But this should be an iron-clad rule: Never give that child a snack later because he is hungry.

Family time

It is so tempting to see to the family and then go about your business. This is particularly true of breakfast and lunchtime. But all precious sharing time can be lost if you do this. Demonstrate to your family that you consider mealtime an important event. Enjoy the meal with them. Smile, relax, enter into their conversations.

Breakfast time

Breakfast is of prime importance. One third
of the recommended nutrients for the day
should come at breakfast, and families need
the best send-off you can possibly give them.
Strive for a variety of nutritious foods. And
what a perfect time for the whole family to
gain spiritual food for the day!

Pray with each child

At breakfast encourage children to share a challenge they might face during the day – a test, a difficult friendship, a teacher situation, a football game. A short prayer offered in earnestness sends the child off with greater assurance. This custom fortifies the family for the challenge of the day and teaches children to rely on God for strength and stability.

Make Fridays special

Friday evening meals should be really special. The table should be set with special mats and a different set of dishes used from the rest of the week. A lighted candle could glow at the centre of the table. The family could hold hands during prayer and someone could share something special that had happened during the week.

After dinner

After dinner the children could gather for family night. They could enjoy a variety of activities from guessing games to musical items and dramas. Perhaps Bible stories could be acted out by the children.

Sleep:
a priority

The best way to get a
good start in the morning
is to get a good night's
sleep the night before.

Sort through the clutter

'There is a time to keep and a time to throw away.'
Ecclesiastes 3:6, NIV

A normal household has more than 3,500 items in it. And we use fewer than 15% of them.

Things to throw out

- Watches that no longer work.
- Craft projects begun but never finished.
- Stacks of expired coupons for products you never buy.
- Broken tools and toys.
- Out-of-date medications.
- Scraps of soap.
- Curtains from a former house.
- Books you'll never read.
- Pots from all the plants that died.
- Boxes of unread magazines.

A new addiction

Some suffer from a grave emotional disease called house-blindness. Science can't explain it, but the symptoms are clear. The sufferer grows blind to clutter. Clutter becomes a way of life. It is an addiction.

Face it: much of what is in your house is useless. Get rid of it!

Negative effects

- Clutter affects us negatively in many ways. It robs us of time; we spend a valuable portion of our time polishing, dusting, cleaning and moving it around.

- Clutter costs money. When shopping, remember: When you get that item home, you have to put it somewhere.

- A cluttered house takes more time and effort to clean.

- A cluttered house affects our relationship with our family.

Removing clutter –

Prepares us mentally
and our home physically
to make way for the new,
and to improve our
surroundings.

Getting
and giving

'We make a living by what we get, but we make a life by what we give.'
Winston Churchill

Don't squander time

*'Dost thou love life?
Then do not squander
time, for that's the stuff
life is made of.'*
Benjamin Franklin

A mother's smile

*'Don't fail to make your smile
your children's last memory
as they depart for school.
A ruffled spirit as a send-off
puts the time out of joint
for the entire day.'*
Mrs G. E. Jackson

A sign above the door

'Christ is the Head of this house, the unseen Guest at every meal, the silent Listener to every conversation.'

Home traditions

Children cherish traditions and draw security from them. Traditions tell them that there are things in life that are unchanging, and can always be counted on.

Who rules?

'Blessed is the home where
– God is at home
– and where the Spirit of
Christ rules.'
Theodore Adams

Duty without pain

'Make it a point to do
something every day that
you don't want to do. This is
the golden rule for acquiring
the habit of doing your
duty without pain.'
Mark Twain

The person you might have been

The biggest obstacle to getting your life in order is yourself.

'It's never too late to become the person you might have been.'
George Eliot

Affirmation

Today I choose to put order in my life.
I can and will begin to sort through the
multiplicity of things that clutter my
home and closets. I realise this may
take time. I will keep a positive frame
of mind throughout the process and
reward myself as each room is
completed. It can be done, and it
can be fun!

Inside of us

*'Our true home is inside
each of us. Our houses
are the outward expression
of something we have
already achieved.'*
Alexandra Stoddard

Outside of us

God says,
'Do not fear, for I am with you; do not be dismayed, for I am your God. I will strengthen you and help you; I will uphold you with my righteous right hand.'
Isaiah 41:10, NIV

YOU matter!

God says,
'Can a mother forget
the baby at her breast
and have no compassion
on the child she has borne?
Though she may forget,
I will not forget you! See,
I have engraved you on
the palms of my hands.'
Isaiah 49:15, 16, NIV

How to clean like a pro

Rule 1: Stop the dirt getting in by –

– a mat at every entrance
– keeping carpets shampooed
– stripping and waxing floors.

Rule 2: Keep the bathroom spotless

Bathrooms need a germicidal action and
a disinfectant cleaner. Use the one
recommended for hospitals.

Rule 3: Have the tools – and use them!

Broom. Dustpan. Dry mop. Sponge mop.
Bucket. Window squeegee. Whisk broom.
Furniture brush. Duster. Toilet brush. Vacuum
cleaner. Hand floor scrubbing brush.

CAUTION

There is a difference between striving for excellence and striving for perfection. The first is attainable, gratifying, and healthy.

The second is unattainable, frustrating, and neurotic. It is also a waste of time.

God's assurance

'When you pass through the waters, I will be with you; and when you pass through the rivers, they will not sweep over you. When you walk through the fire, you will not be burned; the flames will not set you ablaze. For I am the Lord, your God, the Holy One of Israel, your Saviour.'
Isaiah 43:2, 3, NIV

Purpose

The fact that you are alive today is proof
positive that God has something for you
to do today.

Hard work is not stressful.

Losing control over your life is.

Ordinary things

*'The true calling of a
Christian is not to do
extraordinary things, but
to do ordinary things
in an extraordinary way.'*
Dean Stanley

The GO principle

The GO principle of work management states that it is more efficient to do as much as possible of one type of work before changing to another. Management specialists have identified a warm-up period when a job is first begun, but before efficiency has been reached. Peak efficiency is dubbed GO (for Greatest Output). In other words, when any task is tackled at one time we work on a higher plateau of GO than the person who jumps from job to job and back again.

Forgiveness

*'Live creatively, friends. If someone falls
into sin, forgivingly restore him, saving your
critical comments for yourself. You might be
needing forgiveness before the day's out.'*
Galatians 6:1, MGE

Carry each other's burdens

'Carry each other's burdens, and in this way you will fulfil the law of Christ.'
Galatians 6:2, NIV

This applies to the home. Every husband and child should help the wife-mother bear the burden of the home. Husbands, wives and children must work together to maintain a common living space.

Co-operation

Exercise a little creativity.
The family will learn
that work can be fun.
What's learned with
pleasure is learned full
measure.

Private time

Jesus said, 'Come with me by yourselves
to a quiet place and get some rest.'
Mark 6:31, NIV

Every woman needs a quiet place where
she can spend time with the Lord – on a
regular basis.

Leisure time

Leisure is as good for you as are vitamins and sleep.

You owe it to your work, your family and yourself to take time out for leisure activities.

Five-minute leisure intervals

Treat yourself to several five-minute leisure intervals throughout the day.

Now and then we must pause in our pursuit of happiness – and just be happy!

Laughter
IS good!

*'A cheerful disposition
is good for your health;
gloom and doom leave
you bone-tired.'*
Proverbs 17:22, MGE

Underlaughed?

If you aren't laughing twelve to fifteen times a day, you are underlaughed.

'A merry heart doeth good like a medicine' (Proverbs 17:22, KJV) – so go for it!

Detachment

Humour allows us to detach
ourselves from our troubles,
see them in perspective
and, perhaps, eventually
overcome them.

A great tranquilliser

Laughter is a great tranquilliser for problems and stress. Stop being so serious! Start laughing today!

Someone said, 'If you are happy, notify your face!'

Humour

You are never fully dressed
unless you wear a smile.

Laughter is the brush that
sweeps away the cobwebs
of your heart.

Laughter is –

- 'a bodily exercise precious to health'
  (Aristotle)

- 'the closest thing to the grace of God'
  (Karl Barth)

- 'the shortest distance between two people'
  (Victor Borge)

Carpe diem!

Seize the day! Greet today with a smile.
Make up your mind to be agreeable and
make the best of your opportunities.

Start afresh!

Today you have been given a fresh beginning. The world is yours. Enjoy every moment of today – and make them matter.

Open your eyes!

Are you enjoying today? Today you have
been given a new start. Breathe in the fresh,
cool air and revel in the sunshine. Beauty
is God's therapy for the ugly side of life.
Fear, anxiety, depression and worry can be
overcome with an appreciation of beauty.

Today is here

And it is yours.

Act towards God and others as if today were your last day on Earth.

Today is here

Don't think of what you would do if only
things were different. Things are not different.
They are what they are. This is the home you
live in, and these are the circumstances.
Accept what you cannot change – and trust
God for the rest.

Prayer for family safety

O God our heavenly Father, from whom every family in heaven and on earth is named; we trust to your loving care the members of our families, both near and far. Supply their needs; guide their footsteps; keep them in safety of body and soul; and may your peace rest upon our homes and upon our dear ones everywhere; for Jesus Christ our Saviour's sake.
Frank Colquhoun

Prayer for
the family

*Father in heaven, pattern of all parenthood
and lover of children, we pray for homes and
families in this community.
Sustain and comfort them in need and
sorrow. In times of bitterness, tension and
division, draw near to heal.
May parents and children together be learners
in the school of Christ, daily increasing
in mutual respect and understanding, in
tolerance and patience, and all-prevailing
love; through Jesus Christ our Lord.*
Timothy Dudley-Smith

Prayer for family gatherings

Lord, behold our family here assembled.
We thank you for this place in which we
dwell, for the love that unites us,
for the peace accorded us this day,
for the hope with which we expect the
morrow; for the health, the work, the food
and the bright skies that make our lives
delightful; for our friends in all parts of the
earth. Give us courage and laughter and
the quiet mind.

*Bless us, if it may be, in all our innocent
endeavours;
if it may not, give us the strength
to endure that which is to come,
that we may be brave in peril,
constant in tribulation, temperate in wrath
and in all changes of fortune
and down to the gates of death,
loyal and loving to one another.
We beseech of you this help and mercy
for Christ's sake.*
Robert Louis Stevenson

Prayers for the home

May the love of God our Father
Be in all our homes today;
May the love of the Lord Jesus
Keep our hearts and minds always;
May his loving Holy Spirit
Guide and bless the ones I love,
Father, mother, brothers, sisters,
Keep them safely in his love.

Bless our home, Father, that we cherish the bread before there is none, discover each other before we leave, and enjoy each other for what we are, while we have time.

Prayer from Hawaii

God bless the house
From site to stay,
From beam to wall,
From end to end,
From ridge to basement,
From balk to roof-tree,
From found to summit,
Found and summit.
Prayer from Scotland

Home blessing

O God, make the door of this house wide
enough to receive all who need human love
and fellowship,
and a heavenly Father's care;
and narrow enough to shut out all envy, pride
and hate.
Make its threshold smooth enough to be no
stumbling block to children or to straying feet,
but rugged enough to turn back the tempter's
power; make it a gateway to thine eternal
kingdom.
Thomas Ken

A mother's prayer

Lord, I'm so glad
We don't have to be creative geniuses
Or serve elegant gourmet meals
To make our guests feel warm and wanted.
We need rather to expose them to love
And introduce them to laughter.
We need to listen and never drown them out.
Above all, we need to remember
That there is no substitute –
None whatever –
For concentrated sharing
And genuine caring.
Ruth Harms Calkin